Utah

Jim Ollhoff

Visit us at
www.abdopublishing.com

Published by ABDO Publishing Company, 8000 West 78th Street, Suite 310, Edina, Minnesota 55439 USA. Copyright ©2010 by Abdo Consulting Group, Inc. International copyrights reserved in all countries. No part of this book may be reproduced in any form without written permission from the publisher. The Checkerboard Library™ is a trademark and logo of ABDO Publishing Company.

Printed in the United States.

Editor: John Hamilton
Graphic Design: Sue Hamilton
Cover Illustration: Neil Klinepier
Cover Photo: iStock
Interior Photo Credits: Aaron Jack Halls, Alamy, AP Images, Comstock, Corbis, Getty, Granger Collection, iStock Photo, John Hamilton, Library of Congress, Mile High Maps, Mountain High Maps, National Park Service, North Wind Picture Archives, OK State University Library, One Mile Up, Peter Arnold, Salt Lake Bees, S&S Worldwide, U.S. Geological Survey, Utah Blaze, Utah Jazz, and Washington State's Secretary of State Office.
Statistics: State population statistics taken from 2008 U.S. Census Bureau estimates. City and town population statistics taken from July 1, 2007, U.S. Census Bureau estimates. Land and water area statistics taken from 2000 Census, U.S. Census Bureau.

Manufactured with paper containing at least 10% post-consumer waste

Library of Congress Cataloging-in-Publication Data

Ollhoff, Jim, 1959-
  Utah / Jim Ollhoff.
      p. cm. -- (The United States)
  Includes index.
  ISBN 978-1-60453-680-5
  1. Utah--Juvenile literature. I. Title.

F826.3.O455 2009
979.2--dc22
                                        2008052878

Table of Contents

The Beehive State

Utah has snowcapped mountains. It has salty, stony deserts. It has forests. It has river valleys. Utah has a little bit of everything.

The word Utah is from the Ute language, a Native American tribe. It means "people of the mountain."

The first white settlers were Mormon pioneers. Still today, more than 60 percent of the adults in the state belong to the Mormon Church, usually called the Church of Jesus Christ of Latter-day Saints. The Church continues to be a big part of life in the state.

Bees are very busy and they work hard. Utah is sometimes called "The Beehive State" to remind people how hard the early settlers had to work.

Sunrise at Mesa Arch in
Canyonlands National Park.

Quick Facts

Name: The word "Utah" is from the Ute Indian language meaning "people of the mountain."

State Capital: Salt Lake City

Date of Statehood: January 4, 1896 (45th state)

Population: 2,736,424 (34th-most populous state)

Area (Total Land and Water): 84,899 square miles (219,887 sq km), 13th-largest state

Largest City: Salt Lake City, population 180,651

Nickname: Beehive State

Motto: Industry

State Bird: California Seagull

State Flower: Sego Lily

State Rock: Coal

State Tree: Blue Spruce

State Song: "Utah, This Is the Place"

Highest Point: Kings Peak, 13,528 feet (4,123 m)

Lowest Point: Beaver Dam Wash, 2,350 feet (716 m)

Average July Temperature: 73°F (23°C)

Record High Temperature: 118°F (48°C), south of St. George on July 4, 2007

Average January Temperature: 25°F (-4°C)

Record Low Temperature: -69°F (-56°C), at Peter Sink on February 1, 1985

King's Peak

Average Annual Precipitation: 12 inches (30 cm)

Number of U.S. Senators: 2

Number of U.S. Representatives: 3

Beaver Dam Wash

U.S. Postal Service Abbreviation: UT

Geography

Utah has many different kinds of terrain. It has rugged mountains, deep river valleys, hot deserts, and high plateaus. Beautiful rocky bridges and arches are found in the south side of the state.

In the north part of the state is the Great Salt Lake. It is even saltier than seawater. It is a very large lake, covering 3,300 square miles (8,547 sq km). It is also very shallow, averaging only 14 feet (4 m) deep. It is the largest salty lake in the Western Hemisphere.

On the west side of the state is a desert-like area. It is called the Great Basin.

The highest point in Utah is King's Peak. It is found in the Uinta Mountain Range in the northeast corner of the state. King's Peak is 13,528 feet (4,123 m) high.

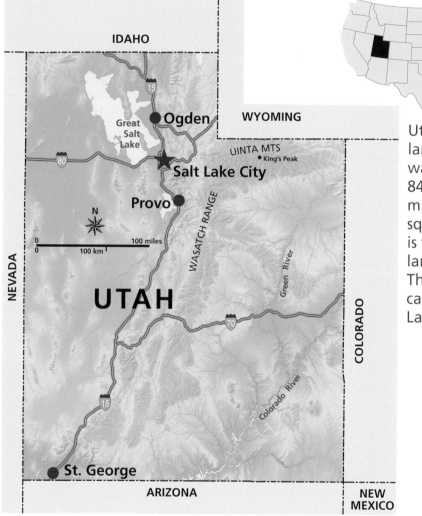

IDAHO

WYOMING

Great
Salt
Lake

Ogden

UINTA MTS
King's Peak

Salt Lake City

Provo

WASATCH RANGE

Green River

N

0   100 miles
0   100 km

UTAH

70

NEVADA

COLORADO

15

Colorado River

St. George

ARIZONA

NEW
MEXICO

Utah's total land and water area is 84,899 square miles (219,887 sq km). It is the 13th-largest state. The state capital is Salt Lake City.

Utah has a stunning variety of rocks. With the rocks come lots of fossils, too. Dinosaur footprints, bones, and even mammoth fossils are found in the state.

Utah is famous for its huge variety of rocks and fossils. Dinosaur footprints from the Jurassic period, 208-146 million years ago, are clearly visible in this rocky area.

In the very southeast corner of the state is Four Corners Monument. Located on

Utah, Arizona, New Mexico, and Colorado meet at the Four Corners Monument.

Navajo land, it is the place where Utah, Arizona, New Mexico, and Colorado meet. It is possible for a person to put their hands and feet in four different states all at the same time. It is the only place in the United States where this is possible.

The main rivers in the state are the Colorado River and the Green River. The Colorado River cuts across the southeast corner of the state. The Green River winds its way southwards from the northeast area of the state, eventually meeting with the Colorado River.

Climate and Weather

Much of Utah is arid, which means it gets less than 10 inches (25 cm) of rain per year. The Great Salt Lake Desert, west of Great Salt Lake, is even drier. It gets less than five inches (13 cm) in a year.

Some mountain areas get more than 40 inches (102 cm) of rain per year.

Utah's Great Salt Lake Desert.

A few areas get more rain than that. Because the state is so dry and mountainous, few tornadoes ever form in Utah.

In winter, the average temperature is just below freezing. Extremely cold temperatures are few and far between in the populated areas. In summer, high temperatures are usually between 85°F (29°C) and 100°F (38°C). The highest temperature ever recorded in Utah was 118°F (48°C), in the very southern part of the state, south of St. George.

Average snowfall in the mountains near Salt Lake City is 500 inches (1,270 cm).

Plants and Animals

Utah has many different kinds of terrain, so there are many different kinds of plants and animals. There are more than 4,000 species of plants. More than 600 species of animals, fish, and birds make Utah their home.

Parts of Utah are covered with dry, salty soils. Many plants grow in these desert areas. Common plants are cactus, yucca, sagebrush, and greasewood. These plants are especially good at growing in desert soils.

Cactus and sagebrush are common in Utah's desert areas.

Many of the mountain areas have forests. The trees in these areas are mostly pines, fir, blue spruce, and aspen. Trees cover about 15 million acres (6 million ha), mostly in the mountains of Utah. Deer, elk, antelope, bighorn sheep, and moose like to live in these areas.

Many animals make their home in Utah's forested areas, including elk.

Mountain lions, coyotes, bobcats, mule deer, and lynx are also found in the state. Wolves and grizzly bears have mostly disappeared from Utah. Bison, also called buffalo, are mostly gone too. There are bison in Antelope State Park. This park covers Antelope Island on the Great Salt Lake.

Small animals can be found all over the state. These small animals include chipmunks, rabbits, squirrels, marmots, fox, and many others.

Utah is a great place for birds. Bald and golden eagles, hawks, owls, and pheasants can be found in the state. Birdwatchers enjoy the annual Great Salt Lake Bird Festival. It highlights the birds on the Great Salt Lake and the surrounding area. The festival has bird workshops, displays, and tours to bird watching areas.

Although shy, mountain lions are found in many areas of Utah.

Bald Eagle

Moose

Mule Deer

History

People lived in Utah 12,000 years ago, and possibly much earlier. The early peoples, called Paleo-Indians, lived in small groups in caves.

Native American tribes moved in and out of Utah through the centuries. About 1200 AD, a group of tribes began to move into Utah. Shoshone, Gosiutes, Ute, and Paiutes all found places to live in Utah. By about 1500 AD, the Navajo and other groups moved into the area.

Pah-ri-ats, a Ute Indian from a tribe living on the western slope of Utah's Wasatch Mountains in 1874.

The first Europeans to see the land may have been two Catholic priests. They and their group were called the Dominguez-Escalante Expedition. In 1776, they set out from Santa Fe, New Mexico, trying to make it to the

In 1776, the Dominguez-Escalante Expedition traveled through Utah.

California coast.

In the late 1700s and early 1800s, Europeans came and went. Most were trappers and buyers. They set up trading posts in Utah.

Fur traders on Utah's Bear River pile their boat high with pelts.

Mormon pioneers enter Salt Lake Valley on July 24, 1847.

One of the most important events for the history of Utah began in Illinois. Joseph Smith was the leader of the Mormons. In 1844, Smith was killed by an angry mob in Illinois. Church leaders realized that they had to leave Illinois, or face continuing trouble. Under the leadership of Brigham Young, the Mormon pioneers left Illinois and traveled west. They came to Utah's Great Salt Lake area in 1847, and decided to make it their home. Thousands of Mormon pioneers joined them in the following years.

There were continuing arguments between the United States government and the Mormons of Utah. The Mormons practiced polygamy, the belief that a husband could have many wives at the same time. This became a big issue.

The people of Utah requested statehood in

Brigham Young led Mormon pioneers to Utah in 1847.

1849. The U.S. government rejected it, largely because of the Mormons' practice of polygamy. The government also thought the church was too involved in Utah's politics.

Utah Territory was created in 1850. By the late 1850s, there were 150 communities in Utah.

In 1865, a series of terrible battles broke out between Native American tribes and the Mormon pioneers. As pioneers settled on Indian land, they cut into the Native Americans' food supply. A Ute chief named Black Hawk led the Native American warriors against the Mormon settlers. Fighting continued until federal troops came in 1872.

The Transcontinental Railroad was completed in 1869. The railroad going west and the railroad going east joined together at Promontory Summit in Utah.

On May 10, 1869, Union Pacific and Central Pacific Railroad officials and employees celebrated the completion of the first transcontinental railroad at Promontory Summit, Utah.

In 1890, the Church of Jesus Christ of Latter-day Saints banned polygamy. Statehood was approved on January 4, 1896. In the early years of the 1900s, Utah adjusted to life as a state. People moved in and cities grew.

In the 1930s, the Great Depression was difficult for the state. However, World War II (1941-1945) helped boost the economy. Farmers sold their crops, and military bases were built.

Utah continued to grow. Research centers, computer technology, and medical facilities all became important in Utah. In 2002, Salt Lake City was the home of the Winter Olympics. This provided a big lift to the economy.

A skater carries the flag of the 2002 Winter Olympics.

Did You Know?

There used to be dinosaurs in Utah. The official state fossil is the *Allosaurus*. This dinosaur could get up to 40 feet (12 m) long. The *Allosaurus* and *Tyrannosaurus rex* were the two big meat-eaters in the dinosaur age. The *Stegosaurus* was also common in Utah. It was an armored dinosaur, with bony plates that stuck up along its back.

Utah's official state fossil is the *Allosaurus.*

Another dinosaur found in the state was the giant *Brachiosaurus.* The combined weight of 15 large elephants equal one *Brachiosaurus.*

More recently, in the last ice age, there were many other animals in Utah. Mammoths and mastodons were elephant-like creatures. *Smilodons,* sometimes called saber-toothed cats, also lived in the state. Ancient camels and horses lived in Utah as well, but all of these animals died out about 10,000 years ago.

Saber-toothed cats, as well as ancient camels and horses, once roamed Utah's lands.

People

BORN
JUNE 1, 1801
WHITINGHAM, VT.

DIED
AUG. 29, 1877
SALT LAKE CITY, UTAH.

Brigham Young (1801– 1877) was born in Vermont, but led thousands of Mormon pioneers to Salt Lake City in 1847. As president of the Mormon Church, he directed the colonizing of Utah. He served as first governor of Utah Territory. He was the president of the Mormon Church until his death at the age of 76 from a ruptured appendix.

Chief Pocatello (1815–1884) was a Shoshone chief. Pocatello was born in northwestern Utah. In the 1840s and 1850s, Mormon pioneers began to settle on Shoshone land. Chief Pocatello led a series of attacks against the settlers. But he finally made peace with them. He tried to help his people as the United States government forced the Shoshone to live on reservations. The government promised to deliver supplies to the tribe, but aid never came. Chief Pocatello worked hard to find ways to help his people. The city of Pocatello, Idaho, is named in honor of him.

Reva Beck Bosone (1895–1983) was Utah's first congresswoman. Born in American Fork, Utah, she became an attorney in 1930. She was elected to the Utah State House of Representatives in 1933. Bosone served as a judge, and was elected to Congress. She served in many important government jobs. In her work, she tried to help women, children, and the poor. She wanted all people to have equal rights to education.

Philo Farnsworth (1906–1971) was the inventor of the electronic television. Born in Beaver, Utah, Philo Farnsworth came up with the idea in high school.

In 1927, Farnsworth transmitted the first image. In 1929, he demonstrated a motion picture. He continued to invent a variety of things, holding 165 patents. He died in 1971 in Salt Lake City.

Robert Redford (1937-) is one of the most famous actors and directors in Hollywood. Redford was born in California, but has lived in Utah for a long time. Redford's acting and directing have won him several of Hollywood's greatest honors, including an Oscar as Best Director in 1981. He is most famous for his movies *Butch Cassidy and the Sundance Kid, The Sting, All the President's Men,* and *Ordinary People.*

Cities

Salt Lake City was founded in 1847 by a group of Mormon pioneers who arrived in the area. They were looking for a place where they could practice their religion in peace. They settled in the area around the Great Salt Lake. By 1869, America's first transcontinental railroad was finished, going through Salt Lake City. Mormon and non-Mormon people settled in the area. Today, Salt Lake City is the capital of Utah, with a population of 180,651.

Utah's capitol building is lit as the sun sets in Salt Lake City.

South of Salt Lake City is the city of Provo. Originally, the area was home to the Ute Indians. Mount Timpanogos

The city of Provo, Utah, sits at the base of several rugged mountains.

and other rugged mountains are visible from Provo. The city got its name from Etienne Provost, one of the early trappers in the area. It is often known as the "Garden City" because it has many trees, gardens, and orchards. Provo is also home to Brigham Young University. Its population is 117,592.

In the southwest corner of the state is **St. George**, with a population of 71,161. It was founded by the Mormons in 1861. The city was named after George Smith, a Mormon leader. He personally selected the pioneers who started the city. Dixie State College of Utah finds its home in St. George. Many retired people come to St. George to escape winter.

St. George, Utah, is close to Zion National Park.

North of Salt Lake City is the city of **Ogden.** It was originally an 1846 settlement called Fort Buenaventura. Mormon leaders bought the settlement in 1847. It was later named Ogden in honor of one of the early trappers. Ogden now has a population of 82,702. Weber State University is located there.

The city of Ogden, Utah, sits at the foot of the Wasatch Mountains.

Transportation

   In 1869, the Transcontinental Railroad was completed. This railroad went from the east coast of the United States to California. It brought the country together. The railroad was built from the east and the west at the same time. The Union Pacific and the Central Pacific Railroads met at Promontory Summit, about 32 miles (51 km) west of Brigham City. On May 10, 1869, a golden spike was driven in, connecting the two railroads and the entire country.

The golden memorial railroad spikes used on May 10, 1869.

Utah's main interstate highway is I-15. From the south, it enters the state near St. George. It travels through the highest population center of the state. This population center, extending from Santaquin through Salt Lake City to Brigham City, is called the Wasatch Front.

Interstate 80 is the major east-west road. It goes through Salt Lake City in the north side of the state. In the south side of the state, Interstate 70 goes east and west.

There are more than 50 airports in Utah, including private airfields and military airbases. By far the state's largest airport is Salt Lake City International Airport.

Salt Lake City International Airport serves more than 20 million passengers yearly.

Natural Resources

Three-fourths of Utah's agricultural products come from livestock. Only one-fourth of the farm products come from fruit or vegetables. There is a trend in Utah, as in other states, of fewer but larger farms.

Utah mines a lot of minerals. The Bingham Canyon Mine is one of the largest copper mines in the world. Gold, silver, lead, and uranium all come from Utah's vast geologic resources. Much of the world's beryllium is mined in Utah. The state is also a major producer of coal.

Bingham Canyon Mine

Utah has 43 state parks, 7 national monuments, 2 national recreation areas, a national historic site, and 6 national forests. There are 5 national parks: Arches, Bryce Canyon, Canyonlands, Capitol Reef, and Zion. Only Alaska and California have more national parks.

Arches National Park

Bryce Canyon National Park

Canyonlands National Park

Capitol Reef National Park

Zion National Park

Industry

When Mormon pioneers first came to Utah in the 1840s, they built an economy from agriculture. They irrigated farmland and grew crops. By 1869, mining was important. In the early 1940s, the United States military built air bases and defense plants. All of these industries still exist in Utah today.

Many crops are grown in Utah.

Computer work and high technology are important to the state. The high technology industry provides 60,000 jobs in Utah. The government and military continue to provide many jobs.

S&S Worldwide manufactures thrill rides.

Manufacturing is a big part of the economy. S&S Worldwide, a maker of thrill rides, and Cephalon, which makes medicines, are large manufacturing businesses. Mining of coal and other minerals bring jobs to the state.

Tourism continues to grow in Utah. Skiing and sightseeing bring money into the state. The Utah economy has many kinds of businesses. This variety helps the Utah economy stay strong.

Skiing brings tourists to Utah.

Sports

The only major league sports team in the state is the Utah Jazz, a team for the National Basketball Association. They have won a number of conference and division titles. They play in the EnergySolutions Arena in Salt Lake City.

Utah has several minor league and development teams. These are teams that give players the experience to move up to major league teams.

The Utah Blaze is an Arena Football League team that plays in Salt Lake City. The Salt Lake Bees are a minor league baseball team in the Pacific Coast League.

Utah also has several college teams that are important, such as the teams from Brigham Young University and the University of Utah.

Skiing is popular in Utah, with a number of major ski resorts. Hiking trails and biking trails also provide outdoor recreation.

Hiking in Utah's national parks is a very popular activity.

Entertainment

Utah is a land of festivals. There are festivals for hot air balloons, trees, birds, eagles, and chili. There are Greek, Asian, and Renaissance festivals. There are book, film, and pumpkin festivals. Art and music are highly celebrated in the state.

Ogden Valley Balloon Festival in Eden, Utah.

Days of '47 float.

One of the biggest festivals is the Days of '47. It celebrates the 1847 pioneer settlement of Utah.

People enjoy parades, rodeos, reenactments, and other activities. The Days of '47 end with all-day activities on July 24, a state holiday.

Robert Redford speaks to a crowd gathered for the Sundance Film Festival in Park City, Utah.

Another famous event is the Sundance Film Festival. Films from new writers and producers are shown. It is a chance for new and independent films to get noticed by Hollywood. The Sundance Film Festival was started by Utah resident Robert Redford in 1978, with the hope that more movies would be filmed in Utah.

Timeline

1300 AD—Native American tribes of Ute, Paiute, Goshute, Shoshone, and Navajo emerge in Utah.

1776—The Dominguez-Escalante Expedition seeks a new route from New Mexico to California. On their way, they explore Utah.

1826—Fur trader and explorer Jedediah Smith leads an overland expedition to California. They travel through Utah.

1847—Under the leadership of Brigham Young, the Mormons arrive in Salt Lake Valley.

1850—The United States Congress creates the Utah territory.

1865-1868—The Ute Black Hawk War is the last major Indian conflict in the state.

1869—The Transcontinental Railroad is completed, with the final spike pounded in Utah.

1896—Utah becomes the 45th state in the Union.

1919—Zion National Park is created. It is Utah's first national park.

2002—The Winter Olympics take place in Utah.

Glossary

Beryllium—A somewhat rare, grey metal that is both lightweight and strong. It is often used in combination with other metals, such as copper, to create a stronger material.

Black Hawk War—Beginning in 1865, the Ute tribe, under Black Hawk, led a series of battles with white settlers. It was the last major Indian conflict in the state.

Church of Jesus Christ of Latter-day Saints—Followers of Joseph Smith. Brigham Young became the leader of the Mormons after Joseph Smith died. Followers of the Church are sometimes called Mormons.

Dominguez-Escalante Expedition—Fathers Francisco Atanasio Dominguez and Silvestre Velez de Escalante are the first Europeans to explore Utah.

Four Corners Monument—The place where Utah, Arizona, New Mexico, and Colorado meet.

Great Salt Lake—A large, salt-water lake in northern Utah.

Mormons—Followers of Joseph Smith. Brigham Young became the leader of the Mormons after Joseph Smith died. The Church is also called the Church of Jesus Christ of Latter-day Saints.

Polygamy—The practice of a husband having more than one wife. Early Mormons had this practice but banned it in 1890.

Shoshone—A Native American tribe that lived in Utah before European-Americans settled.

Ute—A Native American tribe that lived in Utah before European-Americans settled.

Index